Also by Daragh Breen

Across the Sound; shards from the history of an island
(November Press, Cork, 2003)
Whale (November Press, Cork, 2010)

What the Wolf Heard

Daragh Breen

What the Wolf Heard

Shearsman Books

First published in the United Kingdom in 2016 by
Shearsman Books
50 Westons Hill Drive
Emersons Green
BRISTOL
BS16 7DF

Shearsman Books Ltd Registered Office
30–31 St. James Place, Mangotsfield, Bristol BS16 9JB
(this address not for correspondence)

www.shearsman.com

ISBN 978-1-84861-496-3

ACKNOWLEDGEMENTS
'The Lighthouses' section first appeared as an online e-Chapbook
with Smithereens Press. Thanks to Kenneth Keating for his careful
reading while preparing the text for that publication.

'1969. Armstrong drags his bad leg' was first published in *The Stinging
Fly*, as were 'Cross-Dressing with Paula Rego', 'A Short History of
Italian Castrati 1587-1737' and 'The Meat Factory'.
'Alice Maher, Through the Looking-Glass' appeared in *Poetry Ireland*.
'Dorothy Cross's "*Everest Shark*"' and 'The Weather that November'
were published in *The Stony Thursday Book*.
'Summer Solstice' appeared in *The Moth*.

Contents

III

IV

For Eileen

1969. Armstrong drags his bad leg across the moon.

In Dingle they are replacing their tarpaulin flooring with carpets. The Hollywood machine is doubling the average fisherman's income by getting them to produce plastic rocks that will make the local landscape look even more desolate for the making of 'Ryan's Daughter'. They waited on the beach out at Dun Quin for four months for an authentic storm, and when it finally arrived it was so unnaturally fierce that the locals, extras in their own clothing, nearly drowned as the cameras rolled.

Four decades earlier, up the harsh Atlantic coast on the Aran Islands, they plaited seaweed into the rock to create a soil in which to plant, as a well-fed English film crew watched on.

7 years after Armstrong, I sat beneath the photographs of the set of 'Ryan's Daughter' in Kruger's as my mother brought the stories of the filming back from the bar and my father let me taste his bitter black pint. Through a rain battered window I could make out the hump of the Great Blasket like a sleeping whale, and I day-dreamed about a life of isolation on the island.

23 years later, as I sat in the shadow of the ruined church beside the hall in which they were screening 'Man of Aran' and listened to you sing your father's song, I began to trace the lineage of my ghosts in the air around me.

I

The Lighthouses

In a small hole in the ground
wasps made a paper skull,
congealing in miniature weirs
as they piled over each other.

To increase the tight cavity space,
the growing nest like a cranium
pressing against flesh,
the wasps carried water from
a nearby puddle, secreted
it against the earthen wall,
then devoured the softened soil
and deposited it outside.

Hundreds of wasps clambered
about the moistened wall,
a shoal tight in a dragnet,
a skull lodged tight in the dark.

Skelligs (High); 1826, inactive since 1870;
Skelligs (Low); 1967, 53 metres, 3 white flashes,
separated by 2.5 seconds, every 15 seconds.

Storms off-shore constantly shed their skins of waves
as the chasing shoals hover beneath the surface
to feed on the scattered debris.
On the coast road to Dun Quin
a white alabaster Christ crucified in the rain
overhangs a sheer cliff
with the grief of waves
keening against the cold stone face below.
A fury of seabirds and gulls rise
from out of the foam-frayed waves
like blown snow
and bring a blush of whiteness
to the cold dark cliff stone
where they rest and wait.

The storm-thawed light is the same distilled light
as that of the travelling cinemas
that once came through here,
a sheet hung against the damp wall of a hall
by representatives of the Lumière Brothers,
Magi of the Second Coming of Light,
breaking an egg-shape of white against a screen
that began to leak human shadows.

This is where the ghosts come ashore,
peeling the noise of gulls from their tired bodies like sleep,
trailing tide-lines of salt
along the winter beaches in their wake.

Mutton Island; 1817, inactive since 1977;
Aran North; 1857, 35 metres, white flash every 15 seconds;
Inishmore; 1818, inactive since 1857.

Morning on Inis Mór, the musty rust smell
of where ocean meets land,
the gauze of drizzle snagging like cobwebs
against the stone walls
and the pre-history muscle-smell of bulls,
creatures that broke free of the water one morning
coming snorting ashore fully formed.

Dusk, just above the horizon,
the sun is the blood-soaked reds
of a foal's birthing sack,
as it torches the water it becomes a bonfire.

The constant wind is a ragged gown
that trails mosses and lichens across the bare rock.
Lone trees, like soft wax blown onto
the wind and stiffened in an instant
by the cold of the night in which they are formed,
keen in the drizzle for their landscape.
Narrow tombs of stone walls stretch their
bones around the tiny fields.
Out on the water, random light plays
on the water's surface like a giant fishing-lure.

Slyne Head; 1836, 35 metres, 2 white flashes,
separated by 2.4 seconds, every 15 seconds;
Slyne Head; 1836, 18 metres, inactive since 1898;
Inisheer; 1857, 34 metres, white light 6 seconds on,
6 seconds off, red light is shown over rocks to the East.

Across the surface of Connemara bogs
damp bricks of turf are domed in small piles
like worm-casts on tide-receding beaches,
in the coffin-still pools they leave behind
the late summer sun sets, spilling its colours
like a fall of Japanese sacred fish.
These colours, these wind-pigments of loneliness
have been gathered by William's brother and
layered onto canvasses of rural horse fairs
and archaeological excavations of circuses
rendered in rancid flesh, the soft mushroom flesh
of the clown's faces, drowned in earth,
their red make-up smeared like haggish Ophelias.

Amongst the hillocks of rusting metal
on the narrow harbour at Rossaveal,
waiting for a ferry to the Aran Islands,
three elderly Japanese women sit patiently
in white wide-brimmed sun hats,
they have come to see where the sun sets.

The low weeping waves at autumn's dusk
slowly drag their grey manes back
towards the lobster pots that the local women's
ghost sons have lowered across
the mouths of the inlets.

Tarbert Island; 1834, 18 metres, white light 2 seconds on,
2 seconds off, red light West over Bowline Rock;
Fort Point; 1841, 16 metres, white flash every 2 seconds,
red flashes to South East.

A murder of currachs, like up-turned
crows' beaks, crowd towards the rocks,
their tarred ribs shining shell-like and black
in the rain, the waves heave their
meagre fish-catches onto salty shoulders,
testing the strength of the long legs
of their thin oars.

Cows were brought out to these small islands
one by one, knocked over first on the beach,
hooves bound and tilted into the bottom
of the currachs, the men straining on their oars
as they manoeuvred through the waves
with these cargoes of meat screaming on their backs.
One island moved their new bull out to
an isolated islet rock and listened to his groaning
all through the night,
his silhouette could be seen cast in the shadow-void of
lightening, and then just as quickly fainting back into
the pursuing thunder's darkening hail.
At dawn they woke to witness the bull
stumbling ashore on the strand, seaweed
dripping from him, having swum the narrow sound.

One of the Blasket Islands' best know airs,
'Port na bPúcai', was borrowed from a
lovelorn male humpback whale
singing beneath a currach.

Bull Rock; 1889, 83 metres, white flash every 15 seconds;
Calf Rock; 1866, destroyed by a storm 27th Nov. 1881.

Throughout the day, a winter's ghost moon
can be seen low in the sky
like a sea-chalked buoy waiting for the tide
of night to give it substance.
A forgotten wall of lobster-pots remains stacked along a pier,
their wooden frames covered in a mesh of patched blue
and orange rope-work, a cobwebbing of fraying lichens.

Solitary trees bend their ragged manes
into the wind and weep for the fishermen
lost amongst the rocks a ghost's whisper away.
The rain begins to move in off the sea,
beaded to the wind like an armour,
the brown mountains have random patches
of snow, like moulting seal-pups,
their old slopes leak white rushes of water like stigmata.
Their hinterland is pocked with the cairns
in which the winter sun sets daily,
trailing fading light across the moist ground
just as the ghost snail drags the shadow
of the salt that killed him.

Out on the waves, Fastnet Rock lighthouse,
its white gleaming marrow of bone straining
amongst the storm waves with the same
infinite resolve as the four ghost elephants
that keep the Rings of Saturn in place,
balanced on their tusks.
The swinging brightness of its light contains the fossils
of all the storms that have trampled through
its breached darkness as it is carouselled
through the winds like a glinting talisman.
The light is silent from without, but within,
there is the constant rage of squalls against glass.

Sheep's Head; 1968, 83 metres,
three white flashes every 5 seconds;
Mizen Head; 1959, 55 metres,
white light 2 seconds off, 2 seconds on;
Galley Head; 1878, 53 metres,
5 quick flashes separated by 2.5 seconds every 20 seconds.

The sea is in its drowning colour,
night can be heard loudly calving storms in its own dark,
the bony dull skull of the moon is struggling
against the black bulk of the clouds.

A crew of fishermen in their frail currach
know that one of them will be re-born
a seal before dawn,
and Harpo Marx is in the Dursey cable-car
swaying in a cabin of weak tin in the November sleet
as he peers through the scratched Perspex,
his nicotine-stained wings stiff beneath his trench-coat
with the haunted Dursey Sound below,
telling anyone that will listen to him that God and all his
angels have flown south for the winter
as the cable-car tumbles towards that tree-less island
shaped like a muddied hoof-print
in the wild snow of the waves,

and then the vision of the badger,
covered in soot,
spilled from night's chimney,
left heaped on the side
of the road as we drove past,
returning from your mother's funeral,
and I was hoping that you wouldn't see it,
but you were alone anyway,
as if wearing a hood of wolf,
and I felt that all that I could do
was to follow you
bearing all the dead things of this world,
and that all that you wanted
was hidden in the earth,
clasped in a solid box of wood.

Fastnet; 1854, inactive since 1904;
Fastnet; 1904, 49 metres, white flash every 5 seconds;
Baltimore Beacon; 1884, not lighted until recently.

After the storm there is a wake-moon,
low, glassy and globular. It has come
to sit with the drowned.
Leaving Sherkin Island in the rain
the boat moves beneath us with a slow pall-bearers'
motion, and Baltimore Beacon is alabaster-like
in the fading wet light above us, a limb-less
torso dragged ashore and resurrected on the cliff-tops.

And with us come the salmon
returning to their ancestral spawning pools
with their inherent memories of snow and ice
encamped there like the announcement
of the death of a king.

And then, like long thin oars, the sun lets down
its light through the thicket of clouds,
a currach on fire,
and birds will be born in this sky
and they will come screeching
from its heat, laying eggs of thunder
amongst the rains
when night finally collapses
on the land.

And then the high-tide comes screaming, washing past Achill. And 24 minutes later it comes howling past Inishboffin, through Tory Sound. 22 minutes later it passes Cleggan, it then swells into Clifden Bay 6 minutes later. In another 2 minutes it is climbing and clambering over the seal-born rocks of Roundstone Bay. And 1 minute on it gathers itself to swarm around Slyne Head, and then 10 minutes later it is washing past the Aran Islands. It is its own shoal, its own pod, pouring on and on…

Down through the rains it slumbers in to Dingle Harbour, and then past the rusting guns and shipwrecked revolutions of overgrown Smerwick Harbour. And then 12 minutes later it is lifting the dead surface of Bantry Bay. And 5 minutes later it raises the dying trawlers of Castletownbere with its twice daily, drowning echoes. And 2 minutes later it passes Schull, shouldering itself on past the white wingless angel that mourns over Baltimore. 3 minutes later it is spilling fish through Kinsale, before it splashes beneath the watchful glare of Ballycotton Lighthouse, having flooded past the industrial ghost pylons and steel ruins of Cork Harbour's forgotten industries. And on it pours, pouring on and on. On and on…

II

What the Wolf Heard

Six dogs trotting,
their heads bobbing slightly,
and an awareness visible
just beneath the flesh,
worn like the shaffron
plate of armour
attached to a horse's head,
as their heads turn slightly
in a synchronized intensification
and lock on something
just out of our vision,

and then they are galloping,
the whole armoury
of their fur moving
slightly out of synch
with their skeletons,
as we begin to scream,
the placidity of the afternoon
ransacked by darting shadows.

Wasps' Nest

The battered wasps' nest remained hanging
delicately from the beam
even after somebody had taken a stick to it.
The lower-half hung in furled curls of paper,
a crucified Christ mournfully looking down
over his beard into the dark below,
the parchment of the nest like a Bible
dragged through the infinitesimally small intestines
of a thousand wasps, and reconstructed
fragment by dried fragment into
this dome of miniature cloisters, spiral
staircases, hidden tunnels, forbidden
libraries, and sealed relic-chambers
that only the heavy black smoke of a hand-held
torch can clear out.

Aberdeen

He was the first boy in Aberdeen
to be shod properly by a farrier,
the up-turned heel of his right foot
clamped against the hard leather
apron of the man, the short nails
hammered into his soft flesh, the
rim of steel flush to the edge, the
farrier's hand running red as the boy
gushed uncontrollable rushes of
blood, unable to lift his freshly
crowned foot, his hobbled hoof
too agonising to lean on as the
farrier grappled with his left leg.

His father had brought him to that
shadow-mottled laneway, leading him
through the rain-blackened granite
streets. He had prayed for a Centaur
during the heavy nine months
through which his wife had carried the
twins, the surviving child holding his
dead brother when they were cut
from the womb. He carried his boy
home, his only living son crucified
across his back, his steel feet clanking
like dead bells as he dragged twin lines
of blood over the black granite cobbles.

The Last March of Barrie Cooke's
'Megaceros Hibernicus'

The twisted briars of the sun
illuminate him as if on fire
within his own birthing-sac,
a fever of bone-work coppiced
on the caul of his skull,
his skin a monkish cloak
recovered from centuries of
encasement in turf.
He falters up the cloud-blackened
bowled mountains behind Sneem,
his crucifix of antlers boat-heavy
on his shoulders, shouldering ever
on out beyond the stone huts
of the dead on the Dingle Peninsula,
and finally down the steps to
Couminole that twist in on
themselves as if Stations of the
Cross, down to where the sun
dies daily, he descends into
this gull-well and echo-chamber
of shriek and wave-slap of
sheer rock, and then,
at last, too heavy to carry
himself any further, he
plunges the flaming torch of
His being into the hissing flesh
of a rising wave, enthralled
by the promise of the
long quiet silence of death.

Benedict Tutty's Icons

On a separate work-bench lies the baited carcass
of a crow, half-ravaged,
as he sets about re-forging the soft
medieval armoury of a hake,
having first removed its toothed mask for
the detail of a crown of thorns.
It becomes metal-born in the forge,
re-forming from a fox-red tar,
then left to cool until beak-hard.

He returns to form the Saviour's crown
that He must bear on the Cross
that His father made him climb,
from the tooth-mask of the hake
that gapes with the same strangled despair
which a young male fox faces when
forced first by its mother from the den,
and then driven from her urine-staked territory
with an open mouth of saliva-dripping teeth.

Cross-Dressing with Paula Rego

We made leather rabbit headgear
out of discarded calves' heads,
a smirk of lipstick across the
dried, dark, gummy mouths
to mimic nights of red wine,
stapled Victorian clothes to
our chimneysweeps' bones,
carried pigs' heads handbags beneath
giant black-beetle shell shawls.

We strangled each other as we
gave birth to long knives
under dead milk moons
on the animal of our backs,
having lived our childhoods
secreted in brown leather suitcases,
hidden from the wet nurse,
whose dead wings clung like
unborn creatures on the lumpy
rolling skin of her fleshy back,
and her naked tobacco breasts hung
flat against her shrivelled, exposed lungs.

For we are all born from
the one hag's hunchback
and we will all drown in
the dank river in which she bathes,
and if you go down
to the woods tonight
you'd better not go alone,
and if you go to sleep tonight
you'd better go in disguise.

Alice Maher, Through the Looking-Glass

February's looking-glass moon is low
and makes a paper screen of our bedroom window,
and every time a car passes down the lane
its headlights drag the hedge's silhouettes
across the back of the curtains,

widows' ivy regurgitated from the throat
of a toad-licker in a battered wooden shed,
up to her oxters in a gin-bath
and her hair that won't stop growing
snow-deep all over the floor.

They say that she has a retinue of trained otters
at her beck and call, that sleep in the
lake of her hair all winter long,
and every summer they burn willow for charcoal
so that she can continue to render their world.

Dorothy Cross's *'Everest Shark'*

When the world was folded-up
and put away
all that was left behind,
suspended in the void,
were the whales that couldn't
be shifted, three or four
sodden giant deltas that
wouldn't lift, and Everest
like a spill of icing left
to harden overnight, yet
younger than her shark
and its miniature mountain fin
that lies rigid on the gallery floor,
the world laid-out
across its dead back.

When it's left to overnight in
the darkened gallery
the bronze returns to its
earliest state,
a metal crudely cast in the
hollow of hillside stone,
a stalled world, waiting to evolve.

Dorothy Cross in the Waterworld

When she first entered a river at Pendle
the River-God staggered from his watery hearse,
his autumn-broken wings of sycamore quivering
as he lifted her segment of river like a
brood frame eased from a bee-hive, revealing her
squirming form incubating harvest-moon reds.

Stepping from a rusting shed in Fountainstown
she entered the water shielded in a shredded
shark-carcass, its underbelly gilded gold and
burnishing her surrounding waters childhood hues,
a colony of bees swarmed from her wounded side
like a movement of fire just beneath the surface.

While clad in cow-hides in a Connemara stream,
she spawned a god-less season that could
only be brought to an end when she was framed
in the stone-walled colosseum of Aran's Worm
Hole, crucified milky-white against
the inky Stabat Mater of the Atlantic.

Witch Hazel

It grew from out of
the nest of moss she'd swallowed,
in the warm pit of her stomach,
struggling up through
the gullet and throat,
eventually protruding
out of her mouth.

During the first winter
she plaited it through her hair,
and in late June she made
a veil of it across her eyes.

It continued to grow,
forming a train that swept
clear her trailing wet footprints,
snagging at the pedestrian barriers
under the flyover, unformed
fledglings falling to the pavement
as her movements stuttered.

As the overall weight of it grew
her feet slowed, debilitated
by the all-subsuming
form that cocooned her.

She finally came to rest
along the South Ring Road,
the persistent traffic
a heart monitor
reassuring her pulse,
the rain gentle as
a nurse tending her hair.

Four Crows

Standing beneath
the slow rising stretch
of the inked laws of four crows,
it's hard not to re-imagine
a time when local wolves
were asked to be god-parents,
and a she-wolf,
hidden in the hollow
of a dead oak tree,
was given the last rites by a priest,
her pelt half-peeled back
to reveal the aging woman
weeping within.

Under winterwolf skies
in County Cork,
their territories once measured
out in wolf howls,
these four crows know
that those transformed into
wolves for fealty were to be
excluded from the extermination,
so they drag the cloaks of their
croaking around themselves
and resume their constant search
for their retainers, the Carrion Lords
with whom they once feasted.

White-Tailed Eagle, Shot (Tipperary)

50 pellets, like un-strung rosary beads
soldered along its undercarriage,
the lead that once studded
the Medieval night sky
prized free and spat
from a shotgun,
the Guernica of its pain
a flare's sparking fall
with no-one to notice,
and the boards of its
cruciform wingspan
the length of the man
holding it aloft
in his blue overalls
for the photographer.

With a broken wing and
a broken leg, it had come
to ground, for days hunkering
on a haunch as it hunched up
in its own agonised recovery
position, left to slowly
starve to death.

Summer Solstice

The first river died that June.
The eels, as fat as horses,
crowded the river bed
having drank it dry.

The new river arrived in the town
on the back of five lorries,
cross-sectioned in five enormous wooden crates,
covered in tarpaulin.
Everybody followed it down their one street
thinking that it was the Circus,
but it was just water.
None-too-clear empty water.
That night, one of the boys from the back-lanes
crept under the tarpaulin and,
unable to find his way out of the blackness,
drowned.
The local Landlord decided to send the river back.
The next evening a two-man travelling show
arrived in the town and set up their small tent
on waste ground,
charging the town-folk to see a taxidermist
neatly fit a crow's face over his partner's,
4-inch needles holding it in place,
tight as if the scalp had slipped downwards,
blinding her with its awkward darkness,
the sad useless bone of the beak jutting outwards.
To the back of her head he fitted a bonnet of wings.
The local priest was called for
and their tent was later set fire to.

Some boys from the top of the town
found the crow's mask and stitched it onto
a piglet's face and led it down their one street
on a lead, blood pouring in a circle from
the creature's head.
Three young girls vomited on the side of the street.

All that month the sun just wouldn't go down.

Eventually, a pack of parched crows attacked
the swollen flesh of the eels and their waters
broke and released the river.
Once more the moon had a vanity in which
to look at itself.

A Short History of Italian Castrati 1587-1737

His mind North as always
during the hour of the wolf,
the club-footed Medici Prince
was watching the muscle-flow
of his favourite Alsatian,
like the cloak-movement
of a river of starlings.

He lay slumped in his chair,
red wine spilling over his own groin,
saddened by his decision
to have it castrated so as
to preserve its soprano-bark,
before it broke its confines
like a river choking its estuary.

A hundred and fifty years later,
Italian Alsatian castrati
were banned from the
Opera Houses of Verona
after a club-footed mezzo-
soprano was savaged
to death on stage
by an Alsatian in a wig
and white face-powder.

Subsequent bans followed
in Milan, Palermo and Bologna.
In Venice, the final pack of
castrati Alsatians, their fur

matted over the gibbets
of their ribs, were set alight,
the pyre of their gondola
screeching a mutilated torch of agony
down the Grand Canal.

War Horse

He returned from the War with a horse's head
in his suitcase, its eyes cloaked in a cracked cake
of dried mud, its mouth's darkened gums
soldered with the blood with which it lisped
the last of its life.

He wore the hollowed head in bed, the silence
of its chamber dark with the lack of sound,
its enormity resting on the new pillow that his wife
made to accommodate it. He was woken nightly
by his wife's screaming, she waking to this trench-
monster beside her.

The priest turned him away from the church
one May Sunday when he had arrived up the aisle
awkward and unsteady beneath the blinding
horse's head. The priest flicked holy-water at this
creature as he chased it from the sanctity of his
church.

One summer afternoon they found their only son by
the river, his head a living, rotating crown of midges,
a contraption of glass and rubber-tubes in his hands.
When they managed to revive him, he spluttered
through choked tears that he'd been trying to drown
his own soul, so as to win back Daddy's.

His father told him of how the horse had saved his life.
Its left flank riven by a sabre. Falling on top of him and
burying him beneath it in the deep mud as the enemy
raked the quietened battlefield, killing everything visible.

His father died that winter, succumbing to horse worm-colic. Restless and kicking. Sweating white tide-lines of salty excess. Groaning and twitching. The night of his father's funeral, the boy took to wearing the horse's head.

The Meat Factory

It could be seen across the eight lanes
of the South Ring Road,
through February trees,
a large white sign with the words—
The Meat Factory, Public Welcome.

And in the following weeks,
while trapped every morning in lifeless traffic,
we could see queues of young boys
waiting among the tangle of sheds,
their breath visible even from a distance

as they stood in line
clutching their plastic bags
of freshly gathered frogspawn,
hoping to have it transformed
into all manner of beast.

They will return in late autumn,
after the fetid incubation of summer,
with their receipt stubs in grubby hands,
and all sorts of creatures will be ushered out
stumbling into the quiet light.

Malformed and already malnourished
they will be led with bits of old rope
and tied up in the bits of field,
gravelled with broken bottles,
found on the edges of the outer suburbs.

And winter will find them forgotten
and frightened in its freezing nights,
huddled in abandoned cars
or hidden in the ditches,
wondering when they will be fed again.

And come spring
the boys will begin to queue again,
vague sketches in their tracksuit pants' pockets,
again sitting out the boredom of summer
waiting to see what the factory spawns.

A Bull's Notion

A mirage of starlings
formed and reformed
silhouettes of women
that he used to know
before waking-up one day
alone in this field
with this bull's head
on his shoulders,
unable to rise to his feet
for hours at a time
because of its overbearing
weight, his underdeveloped
legs foal-like in their
stumblings, his feet fumbling
in the mud as the stars
that his mother wept
doubled themselves
in the surrounding puddles.

As the nights passed
his back began to ripen
to accommodate the weight
of his new head,
and, his arms and legs
now larvaed in mud, with
the shadows mutating
into trees that echoed
the wind and the
memory of voice
like another creature
within the leathered

labyrinth of his own skull,
the gathering echoes
birthing the memories
that he was someone's son
were the only thing
that sustained him.

Young Gods

The old Gods
were rivet gun men
with Harland & Wolff,
horse-flesh men
down on Youghal's Front Strand,
men of candle-stubs
and undiscovered hearts.
Theirs was a badger-dark
in which everything
was textured of
black smoke.

Seasonally, they would
take to the woods
to drown their own
Wolf and Great Elk
to see if they'd
come bloated
and witching
to the surface,
the rivers full
of what they'd
laid to waste.

But now they
come ashore,
the young Gods,
stumbling yet new,
echoing of ocean
river and stream,
bearing between them

late October's
harvest moon,
a torch borne into
Winter's Great Hall.

All Hallows

Most mornings,
November's featherless wings
sit among the trees
and the light has
the dull sheen of an echo,
and here at the edge of the world
we peer over the precipice
to see the shimmering glint
of salmon, mackerel and herring-armour
where they sleep among
the briars of tree roots
that make wreaths to nest the stolen light
down the cliff of the Earth's side.
We watch the goats visible further below
foraging on the nearest stars,
and below them again
the heavy force of whales
that have fallen through
the bottom of the oceans
and are rescued and dragged like Zeppelins,
back to the portholes they'd made,
by the giant skulls of turtles
that patrol the lowest levels.
And then, dizzied by what we've seen,
we walk back across the field,
our footfalls crushing the grass
stiffened by night's cold shed-skin
and we wait for tomorrow's early fall of dark
when we again walk the edge with the dogs
to ensure that the month's herded dead
haven't stumbled out into the oblivion.

The Weather That November

We were encoded by
the weather that November,
when the white gauze of the air
eventually lifted
to reveal a light
that had seen better days
heaped and pooled in the ditches.

Then we listened for hours to the
wind inside the wind inside the wind
beneath those falling skies,
only later to be watched
by the Sheela-na-gig moon
as it leered at us
from behind the trees.

The Crowning of Mr. Punch

At Wolf-Cathedral they found
a crude effigy of Mr. Punch as Christ,
his large carved nose looming
down over the rutted ditches of
of his torso, his dark nostrils leaking
drippings of painted blood.

A Wolf-Church they discovered
a soot-stained altar fresco
of a pieta depicting an un-hooded
Jack Ketch, the Hangman,
his body buckled and draped across
the lap of a mournful Judy.

At Wolf-Rock they unearthed
an engraving showing a hunched
Mr. Punch astride a wolf,
riding into a shattered town, his heart
a tangled-briar of thorns that had been
worn tight around his hat-less skull.

Dead Bees

The spitted lamb,
its four limbs tied-off with wire,
and the jelly of its underbelly
split as if slowly unzipped
as it calves
from its newly sundered halves
a foam of dead bees,
an apron of fur
that begins to unfurl itself
like a spill of mossy entrails.
When they are removed from the flame
they will harden into
a striped wax
that will be combed free
into a bucket
to be fed to the waiting ewes
in which they will ferment
and give life to themselves once more.

Six white sky lanterns
come wobbling
out of the solid dark
like soundless bells,
their bobbing, slurring
hollow shells
reverberate their own
trapped light,
ghost skulls
of ghost wolves
unsteady in their new world.

They have been condemned to
a purgatory of lunar years,
become concubines to storms,
but with no miles of endless hair
to sit combing out
as the Earth
takes an eternity
to die.

III

Requiem for Ned Kelly

1. Professional Wolf Hunters

We'd been read the reports
of how they'd come from
out of the sea of the night,
the foliage of their dreamings
like an autumn
mapped out in their wake,
and we'd been commissioned
to be the cartographers of their extermination,
filling hulls with their pelts and skulls
for the big Halls of our homeland.

We dragged our grim chains
behind our giant wolfhounds,
their musket barks
bringing death to every forest
through which they echoed.
We hung bones in the dark,
death-chimes against
the Pope's witchery,
his animals spying on us
throughout winter's months of dusk.

We could not light fires
and so prayed to the dark stale-
cloth of our own faith on Sundays.
That land of devil-creatures
frightened us,
we will never go back
for we have heard too many
chambers of night
echoing with the silver screams
of its people's flying souls.

2. The Death of a Wolf

So many ghosts here tonight.
As a slow river of deer antlers
moves black and tangled
across the Tipperary snow,
the wolves have left their heaped
furs aside to walk through
the fires that the men have lit.
In the red bonfire light
the men plot out the routes
that the newly dead
must follow as they
ford the silting dark.

Night had left a bark
of frost on the dead wolf
where he lay in the
dark-ridged muck,
his fur the colour of
a dying bonfire.
The sleepless river that
drove his skull
ever-on-wards
has scuttled itself, succumbing
to the gravel and silt of
its dominion of night.

3. Young Ned Saves a Boy
from Drowning

The old woman, her face shadowed
by passing wings, hunkered to wash
grave-clothes on the gravel bank,
then stalled at her work to watch
as a boy crawled into the water.

And she continued to watch as
an 11 year old young Ned
wrestled a small body from
the river's sway, a lush wetness
inking its darkening fur, four
limbs clambering for solid ground
as it was carried ashore, a dingo
shaking itself dry in wings
of spray on the gravel while
young Ned lay on his back, grasping
at the blinding sun for air.

4. Young Ned Suffers a Vision of a Bonfire in Tipperary

On Bonfire Night
all the local boys gathered in masks
made from old fishwives' tails
in the forgotten open-air butchery
of the abandoned shambles
on the hill from which blood used to run
in ribboned rivulets between the cobbles.

And from behind the flames
stamped the one chosen to be that year's wolf,
five long knives dangling
from the bowed and buckled scruff
of his neck,
the hand of a metal God made visible
to all present.

Tonight, the last of his innocence
will be flensed from him
and in the morning
he will wake beside the ashes
of his childhood
with a metal bucket secured
to the blinded weight of his head.

5. At Stringybark Creek

At Stringybark Creek Ned first heard
the universe ringing out his name,
and felt himself clattering inside it
like a clapper, as it trailed a spark
of stars across night's near sky.

And he felt doomed to paralysed silence
by the knowledge that he was part
of the anatomy of the bell that
would calve his own assassin, and that
his Undertakers were ever nearing
with the packhorse to which
they wanted to strap his body.

6. An Angel Speaks to Ned About Armour

Constructed during a distant crow-hooded winter,
this will be the coffin in which you are born,
and blindly you will trawl the crawl-space
of your personal catacomb.

You will wriggle to your death
in this pinched and sealed capsule,
a sealed casket genetically embossed
with its own ghost-code.

7. 97 lb. of Battered Ploughshare

When Ned Kelly stepped down
from a Glenrowan hotel at dawn
into the Australian June mud,
strapped inside
the shambolic metal carcass
of 97 lb. of battered ploughshare,
he'd already been dead for three days.

When the authorities
removed the jaw-less tomb
of his metal helmet,
what they found
was the dingo's head
that his Mary had substituted
for poor, dear Ned's.

8. The Sun, the Moon, the Stars, a Noose for Ned Kelly

When the stars were unbolted
and the re-enforced steel of the
moon removed,
a tangle of harvest-rot was fitted
around the mildewed sun
that hung
like a dead hive
over dawn's dead land
that was now prepared
to return to a time
before the naming of things,
before it was laden with
the cargo of Convict Ships,
when this continent belonged
to just the sun, the moon
and the stars.

9. Sidney Nolan's Ned Kelly

When he was a child
his mother had led him to believe
that he could hear
what the last wolf in Ireland heard;
the sound of night's ship being launched.

As he moved across the deep-red South
he was now only battered metal,
assembled from primitive farm machinery,
alien to the alien sun
balanced on his Palm Sunday mount.

And when the sun is rolled back
to reveal the flat red sleeping expanse
there will be no body to be found,
just five sheets of battered and beaten metal
defeated by the land.

10. Plainsong

Across the flat Australian night
dingoes howl at the ghost-light of stars,
and the tanned hide of the land
releases its own ghosts.
as the marsupial clouds
reveal their monthly moon
and give light to the semi-armoured
form of Poor Ned,
who buckles beneath
its weight as the empty
landscape around him
echoes with the
Convict Ship nightmares
that have been woken,
only to find themselves here,
lost among another race's
ancestors' dreamings,
of which they can
comprehend absolutely nothing.

11. The Re-Introduction of the Wolf

Just as a tree echoes once a year
against the shelter of its own bark,
a silent bell marking-off time,
so the winter solstice stalls the Earth
as the clockwork of night is reset
and every well, gibbet, stock and
coffee shop is secured
as the wolf comes
with his lazy-limbed shuffle
of honey spilling and slipping
from a honey-spoon.

There is a bell-less plait of bees
swinging from his neck
as the inflamed memory
of his forced extermination
melts like a cascading slide of wax
inside the hive of his lunar-forged helmet.

IV

Sun King

I. Low Winter Sun

The piled crubeens and disassembled meat parts
of a great bull, arranged and displayed above
the corridors of stagnant algaed water,
that cobble the memory of the English Market
in the smog and tinsel-fashioned
winter of a Cork childhood, a city baptised with
the residue mess and damp ash that trails a
crow when forced from its hidden chimney nest,
form the armour of memories that we stitch and
daub all about ourselves as we walk into the
blindness of a low winter sun
         as we listened to your childhood
stories, and your great wish that the four of us
would always remain secured in brotherhood
            and never end up like Cū, the boy
born of a hound, who pierced the armour-flesh of
his half-brother Fer Diad's welt-hardened skin
of crubeen pig-hoof, causing the sour blood of the
Dark Bull of Death to ooze free as its giant form
manifested itself in the ford, and all four provinces
shuddered with the knowledge that something
that could not be contained had been set free.

II. Tabernacle

February is the month of Patrick Scott sunsets.
Leaving the city, returning home from work
on the road to West Cork, and the black
sod of the impenetrable sky easing free
the lower half of a disc of sun
that seems to sit, momentarily, perfectly
on the horizon,
           a seasonal Tabernacle pried open
for the storms of the coming weeks
that will hopefully take with them some
of the towering leylandii along our south ditch,
saving us a few weekends worth of work,
and let the low future suns of winter
gleam their way to us above the next field
                that never fully dries out,
and over which the morning fog always
seems to linger. These sunsets let the
beasts that we are know that we are
about to be released from winter's
labyrinth, and led stamping into the new
storm-light.

III. Good Friday

The sun, as always, sets just off the stone-rubble
of Connemara, dragging with it the dark from
just beyond Mars, drowning all the fuchsia-clogged
lanes of childhood summer evenings out along
Dog's Bay,
        and Clifden also topples into the dark,
only its rooftops visible in the moonlight, like
the jellyfish that cobbled the coast's warm beaches
and across which we step once more into the hotel
hallway where you once lead the four of us
to look at the photographs on the wall of
Alcock and Brown who made that first Trans-Atlantic
flight in what looked like a homemade aeroplane of
lashed together tarpaulin, travelling sightlessly
through the Atlantic night.
            Some morning saw us rumbling
towards the flaming pyre of the sun as it coloured
the inside of the plane the yellows of the gorse
that smells of the cheap macaroon bars that you
loved so much, talking about Little Richard, Jerry
Lee Lewis and Midfield Generals,
        and in this ford of your memories
I realised that someday the same Dark Bull would
trample free of its stall and come snorting across
the sea of clouds, coming ashore in the weakening
mind.
           Yet, I have seen you now as a man,
a youth, a young boy, and when all our collective
years have slipped from us, drip by slow-slow drip,
and lie pooled in the universe's stilled dark silence,
the spaces where we sat or walked or talked

will remain, like hollowed-out ghost forests,
waiting for some future sun to nest in their
wide, bridging arms.

Lightning Source UK Ltd.
Milton Keynes UK
UKOW03f0044070117
291531UK00001B/38/P